CU00376690

. . . indeed a very personal statement with others. About finding peace throug yourself (and God). There is beauty in I see elements of Zen and Mindfulness.

— Dan Arler, former CEO of Electrolux EMEA

. . . you lead into reflection on one's own behaviour and thoughts. Always, you show a way of life. . . . A thought came to me: perhaps the contemplation you share is a contemplation of Christ as the Way?

— Dom Xavier Perrin OSB, Abbot of Quarr Abbey, Isle of Wight, UK

The unabating noise that surrounds life in the 21st century can cause us to become distracted and numb to what is most important, connection. Whether that be connection to myself, connection with others or, most importantly, connection to the current moment. I find these short stories and reflective passages from Jake to be the perfect tonic. I can dip in, take a breath, reflect, and reset.

— Luke Harding, Managing Director Electrolux UK & Eire

To be in relationship is to be human; to be human is to be in relationship. Jake explores the essence of our humanity through this lens. With clarity, beauty, and longed-for simplicity, he offers observations and questions that allow the reader, his friend, to move inward and touch the peace and resonance of inner knowing. And then, take it back out into the wild world of living and leading.

— Dr. Kim Smolik, Executive Partner, Leadership Roundtable, USA

SEEN

contemplations shared

Jake Esman

SEEN

Published by Beyond the Mechanics,
Isle of Wight, United Kingdom

www.thewayover.com

Cover design by Chris Hall

Photography by Amanda Herbert

ISBN: 978-1-3999-4099-3

Printed in the United Kingdom

CONTENTS

SEEN

contemplations shared

Be still and know that I am God

Ps.46:10

PRO DEO

My friend Raffaella said to me, *You can call it* Chance, *I call it* God, s*ame thing!* as she laughed heartily. If you struggle with the term *God* feel free to read *Love, Light, Truth, Me, Presence, Energy, Chance, Luck* or whatever else works for you. I write for God, because I know I am only a vessel and that nothing is possible without Her.

This realisation that nothing happens because of me opened me. It is something I have always known but never quite dared to own. Then came a burnout. God made me stop, and not just a little bit. I crashed. I was lost and incapacitated. I remember thinking that I would use my time away from work to do more running, my passion at the time. I put on my trainers and left the house. Five minutes later I stopped dead in the middle of the woods and walked home. I wanted to run, but I couldn't. God had stopped me (I did not know that back then). I needed to be stopped. I had not been listening — for too long. That is where things started to change, slowly.

À la claire fontaine m'en allant promener

J'ai trouvé l'eau si belle que je m'y suis baignée

Il y a longtemps que je t'aime, jamais je ne t'oublierai

Sous les feuilles d'un chêne, je me suis fait sécher

Sur la plus haute branche, un rossignol chantait

Il y a longtemps que je t'aime, jamais je ne t'oublierai

Chante, rossignol, chante, toi qui as le cœur gai

Tu as le cœur à rire, moi, je l'ai à pleurer

Il y a longtemps que je t'aime, jamais je ne t'oublierai

J'ai perdu mon ami sans l'avoir mérité,

Pour un bouquet de roses que je lui refusai

Il y a longtemps que je t'aime, jamais je ne t'oublierai

Je voudrais que la rose fût encore au rosier

Et que mon doux ami fût encore à m'aimer

Il y a longtemps que je t'aime, jamais je ne t'oublierai

— traditional French song

PREFACE

I have come to realise that I love learning in connection with others. In deep conversation we help each other to make sense of the world. My work happens mainly in dialogue with individuals or groups. To me it is all about being as real as I can be and trying to meet people in their humanness.

I spend most of my working day talking with people. Sometimes only listening is required; sometimes we discuss. My objective is to create perspective. There is no one solution, no one answer, no one truth. There is only your truth, which is the one that will shape your actions. If we can get perspective on our truth, we can reshape how we act.

I talk to people about their relationships. We use the term *leadership*, but if you think about it, it is all about relationships.

My relationship with myself and my relationship with others largely determines how meaningful my life is. When my life is meaningful to me, I believe in my actions.

How do we create a space for conversation where we can get past the chatter that merely tries to obfuscate what is truly going on? How do we let our interlocutors know that it is okay — necessary even — to say what we feel?

Let's go for a wander along all the things that we know. I want to remind you of truths that you and I may have forgotten.

When I speak to you about leadership, please know that I am not speaking of hierarchy. Leadership is everywhere, accessible to anyone. Leadership is the art of seeking, the art of *right living*. Right living is seeing what is truly important for you, what truly gives meaning to you in this short mortal journey. It differs from what others desire; its essence is the same. To establish what it is, we must start seeing things for what they are, rather than what we think they are.

We can live by emulation, following the examples of those who have inspired us. But there is a risk that what we choose to emulate is not who we are. The acknowledgement of our true self is the cornerstone for acting from source.

I am aware that we are in the age of information overload, and I often feel unsure whether I should give someone a gift as time-consuming as a book. This collection of texts has been written with this concern in mind. I have written short texts and verses that can each stand on their own and that I feel are relevant to the conversations I have with the people who I meet. My hope is that you will read and, more importantly, reread this book when you realise that you need to stop for a moment to get a little perspective or some spiritual refreshment. Sometimes, more often than you think, stopping makes all the difference.

I do not pretend to have written anything of any literary quality. I have merely attempted to articulate what I see in the hope that it may be of help or of comfort.

Finally, as to the title of this book: I have written what I have seen; I have allowed myself to be seen, and I want you, the reader, to know that you are seen.

SERVICE

When we lead we create new realities, realities others can connect to. Our objective is to move the system into a direction that has more impact. For that we must not only speak, we must mostly listen. We have to listen to our surroundings, the context we operate in. It requires a high sense of awareness. To be fully conscious, we need to ensure we are composed, poised and attentive. If we are too concerned with our personal needs we lose sight of the bigger picture, *the field*. If we want to be effective leaders we must be thinking in terms of the bigger system, of everyone and everything involved or affected.

Our growth as human beings, as leaders of our lives, is not in what works for us, or what we do well, it's in the stuff we don't like, the stuff that doesn't go so well, the people we don't like so much.

When I say that I want to be a good person, a person who acts respectably, who is an example to his children, then I cannot selectively exclude the feelings that are inconvenient for me — my dislike of a colleague, my annoyance at my neighbour, my anger at the shop assistant. Sure, things go wrong all the time, but that is not the point. The point is that I try to do what is within my power and accept what is not within my power. And when I get it wrong, I need to dust myself off, pick myself up, try again and move on. What is important is that I own my reality. Dismissing someone because they irritate me, because I find them stupid or arrogant is too easy. When I dismiss someone, I am simply trying to avoid the challenge of making something work. When I acknowledge what I struggle with, what I am not good at, and enter the challenge of at least trying to shift this, I am entering into the possibility of growth. This growth is not a certainty, but at least we have possibility. Leadership is about believing in possibility, in daring to hope. When we become cynical, we deprive ourselves of that hope.

If you want to be successful, it is key to understand that nothing is about you. When we start to look at how we can be of service, we start to uncover what is meaningful. We serve within the limitations of our abilities and sometimes we stretch our abilities to be able to serve. The fact that we serve with what we have and who we are, makes what we do *ipso facto* meaningful. A meaningful life is a successful life. It is beyond possessions, money or achievements; it simply is.

RELIGION

I was recently speaking to Chris, a beautiful Glaswegian in his forties and a fervent practitioner of mixed martial arts (MMA). In this sport, people fight until one person taps himself out. This is usually at the point where the opponent has such a grip on you that he can either break one of your limbs or suffocate you.

When Chris was talking about his weekly MMA practice he was glowing. He said that he loved the intensity and the attitude that is required for this:

You really need to get stuck in. The people who show up for this kind of thing come from all walks of life: builders, plumbers, butchers, lawyers, bin men, teachers . . . What makes it so special is the camaraderie we have between us. It is probably triggered by the fact that we need to trust each other a lot. Your sparring partner can damage your body if he is not careful, and this can have very long-lasting consequences. Going there is good on several levels: the physical, the mental and something else . . .

That *something else* is our spiritual food. The feeling we get when we are in true connection with others, when we know we are dependent on them, when we realise that what we are doing cannot be done without them. So, I offered to Chris that this was sort of his religion. He smiled.

When people come together and experience that what they are doing cannot be done alone, we basically start to touch on the realisation of our interdependence, that we are nothing alone. *Religion* comes from the Latin *religare* which means to *bind* and from *ligare* to *unite in harmony*. When we get married we are ritually united as a couple where each cannot exist without the other (well, you can, but you would not be a couple).

If I think of this story in the context of teams, it still surprises me when leadership team members drive their own agenda without considering the overall result. What's the point of an excellent marketing campaign if supply chain cannot deliver on the demand you have created?

Nothing makes much sense if we do it just for ourselves. The result is meaningless, it serves no purpose and will leave us feeling empty. When we know that what we are doing is part of something bigger we feel united, we feel connection.

That is why it is so important to be aware of our interdependence. When we don't feel united and connected; what then? That is the moment that we need religion — or at least a way, a ritual to *re-bind*. That also goes for leadership teams.

Imagine practising mixed martial arts on your own . . .

APPROPRIATE RESPONSE

Our acts range from completely selfless and beautiful to heartless, nasty and destructive. We like to think this is not so and we prefer to consider the dark side of human nature a phenomenon that occurs in others. The reality is that we are all capable of all the good and all the bad stuff.

Many of my actions are defined by my biography, my upbringing and my context. This reality helps me to understand that I may not always know what triggers me, but I can observe that it triggers me. And when I am aware of this, I have the possibility to step into it and shape my response. In every situation — especially challenging ones — I can ask myself: *What is the right response?* Doing this automatically gives me agency.

We respond to something or someone. When I respond to something there is also a human being involved — me. Therefore I equate response to relationship; either a relationship with someone else or with myself. How I respond will generate feelings in others and myself. To find the right response we have to try to imagine how others or I may feel in the situation at hand and how these feelings may evolve as I take action (respond).

The key to this imaginative response is compassion. Empathy helps us to tune in to our and others' feelings. It is important to be able to empathise; this is our capacity to share and understand the feelings of another. But it is only the first step. Compassion is about taking the right action based on what we understand. Empathy on its own is not enough. It is the action we take that turns our empathy into compassion.

empathy is the doorway to compassion

Compassion is not always easy, as the response that we know is right may not always be a pleasant course of action.

Imagine having to tell a colleague that I have recently started noticing that she is overbearing and arrogant in meetings. How will she take the feedback? She may get angry. Maybe it's just better to leave things as they are. Is this the right course of action or am I just trying to avoid a confrontation? Or do I have a responsibility that goes beyond my personal comfort and sense of safety? If I stop guessing and start acting, I may find that I can enter into much more effective and meaningful conversations and relationships.

Leadership is realising that it is not about me. In fact, we are at our most powerful when we realise that nothing is about me. When I step into that reality, when I am selfless, I will find that there is true liberation. When I know nothing is about me, then everything that I do *is* me! Appropriate response at its best is leadership.

Leadership is entering into selflessness. If I can embody selflessness it is easier to find the right thing to do; to be compassionate.

When the Curtain Falls

Know that there is always light somewhere —

perhaps you're just the other side of the curtain.

TRY

In the Western corporate world, the verb *to try* has a poor reputation. We want to *fail fast* to get *to the next level.* Our paradigm is that we can force renewal, innovation and success by just going harder at it.

In a meeting with a small group of spiritual friends, I was told off one day for saying that I would try, for saying it three times. In fact, I was lectured that someone with my confidence and willpower should not be so weak in committing himself. I was surprised. Did the person who gave me the feedback really think that I had chosen my words so carelessly?

I am trying (no pun intended) to live a life that acknowledges that nothing is entirely within my control. I make plans and carry them out, but that does not mean that the outcome is always what I had intended, foreseen, or hoped for. Accepting this is not defeatist; it is realism. And it carries a lot of freedom.

So, according to my friend, I should not *try* to win a game of cards; I should just win it. I should not *try* to convince a business partner; I should simply convert him to my way of thinking. Easy, right?

> *You can't always get what you want.*
> *But if you try sometimes, you just might find,*
> *you get what you need.*
>
> The Rolling Stones

I think that the assumption that we can simply create what we want, exactly as we want it, lacks humility. To be more direct, I think it is short-sighted. We can't possibly know what a good outcome is and there are too many variables in our complex world to decide what is a good or bad outcome.

The fallacy of control leads to disappointment and is too closed-minded to be able to take advantage of the unexpected. Free yourself from that. *Try* and maybe what ensues is more valuable than you could ever have imagined.

WHAT I NEED

When we live and work with others, the difficulty lies in the difference of our needs. What is a good outcome? Getting the other person to do what I want? Having people agree with me?

When we live life with ourselves, what is a good outcome? That I feel good? That I feel good about myself? That everything pans out as expected?

Can I let go of what I think people or things need to be? What does that require? What could that bring?

I just want to avoid disaster. I am simply not prepared to believe that something good might lie beyond the results that I dread.

I was a partner in a firm. We were growing. We agreed terms. Then, what was agreed unexpectedly changed. Or, perhaps, not so unexpectedly; I had simply not been paying attention to what was real and what wasn't. I decided that this meant that there was only one option: to leave. It scared me. I had worked for over five years to help grow this business and now I would lose everything.

Three years later, I am part of a new partnership co-founded with two others. It is a business that is far closer to what I believe in and identify with. The brand has a deeper level of authenticity in relation to me and I know people can feel that.

This is not the first time in my life that I was trying to avoid an outcome that I had dreaded. And it was also not the first time that what came after was actually better.

What is this requirement to not want to break the status quo? What is this assumption that sticking with what we've got is the safer option? Even though there is ample proof that when doors close it is impossible to predict the good or bad that comes after.

we live in fear and anxiety

of the things that

never actually happen

Where is the point in attaching a label of good or bad to the things that happen? I can only see that in hindsight — often much, much later. Yet we are addicted to appraising what happens to us. Why is it better not to do this? It costs so much energy! *This is good, I must celebrate — oops it wasn't . . . This is bad, I am going to have sleepless nights — oh gosh, that turned out to be so lucky; if this had happened then I wouldn't have . . .* and so it goes on.

Can I develop a practice where I defer judgement, where I just observe my situation without judgement? Tricky, yes. Empowering, for sure.

The Wayfarer

When I feel rushed
and anxiety is having its way with me

when I need to go faster for fear of falling behind
and a hand seems to tighten around my throat

I am in the whirlwind of unconsciousness
on a driverless train heading for the abyss

I need to be lucky enough to be reminded
that I can simply stop and breathe

Breath gives me presence
I step into the now

I inhale what is real and let go of
all that I was imagining to be true

COMPOSURE

Composure is a great friend of awareness. If I can stay composed I can respond from my source. I can take the time to contemplate on the best response without flying into the external trigger. I can reflect on the input and deflect the impulse. The impulse is often a first reaction based on feelings like excitement, joy, hope, hurt, fear, frustration, anger, or anxiety.

If I can retain my composure I can still get angry, but only if this serves the situation. I don't want to lose my passion, but my passion has to walk with me rather than me being under the spell of my passion.

Checking my composure helps me regain control; control of the assumption that I need to be in control.

Tree

Patiently swaying in the sea breeze
with no possibility to up sticks
her limited freedom commits her
committed to witnessing the world

what if I stuck at it?
what would happen if
I didn't walk away
against my first instinct?

is limitation a curtailing of one's freedom
or is it an invitation into a reality
not previously imagined,
dismissed as impossible even?

we like avoiding the Cross
denial at its best

we simply don't believe
there is Life after death

the phoenix rises from the ashes
like never before
if I know this why do I keep running away?

PROVIDENCE

Do I dare to let myself fall off a cliff backwards and trust that I will land on my feet? The belief in Providence is closely related to the concept of *Wu Wei*. In Wu Wei you are attentive to every possibility but you never try to push that possibility. Wu Wei is the art of not forcing, of following the development of events and playing your part, yet never trying to go faster than the present. We respond to what emerges. This belief that what emerges is right is an act of faith, or trust if you will.

Living with providence asks us to let go, to understand that it is not we who decide what the future holds. We are players — what we do matters, but what happens is far more complex than that; we are pilgrims who must navigate charted and uncharted territory.

Accepting this requires courage. And as soon as we step into this act of faith, we feel release. The tension that is involved in trying to control what you know is not really yours to control is not sustainable.

So, what do we do; nothing? Certainly not. Attentiveness to what is emerging is hard work; we have to be wide awake, fully aware. We stop looking at what is wrong. We stop looking at what needs fixing. Instead we orientate ourselves toward what we want to expand; what we have that is good that needs amplifying. We step into creation; into seeing all that is possible. Unrealistic? Are there no problems? Sure, but your way of looking will change the balance between problem and possibility.

FREEDOM

If I knew what it was, would I really want it? If I have freedom then I choose what I want — every time. Imagine that! Do I do what I want? What is it that I want? Does it mean that there are no consequences? Does it require financial independence?

Freedom is far greater than that. To be free means that we live in the here and now — not so easy. It means that we take full responsibility for the actions we take, gladly. Freedom means that we don't judge what is good or bad. We live our reality fully, effortlessly. We live in full authenticity, embracing what we know is right. This is not what we know with the head; it's what we know in our whole being. We are what we do; it's in every fibre of our bodies.

Once we are on this path we are on our mission. The mission to bring into the world what only we can bring. Personally, I am not always so sure that I am living this. I wonder if I am still on the right track, or just coasting. I feel the necessity to question myself. I want to make sure that I am still on the way and getting lost is part of the deal. It is about the commitment to keep on searching. It is the life of the seeker; hard and tremendously rewarding.

There are times when I step into victimhood, telling myself that I can't do something. It's not that I should be saying that I can do everything, but it is about the attitude, the perspective of believing that things may be possible and worth trying. Victimhood atrophies; agency expands.

Freedom is about leaning into the resistance, into the constraint or limitation, seeing it as an integral part of the process and trusting you will come up with a way forward. Growth happens when the going gets tough. When, momentarily, we can't see what can be done. We need to draw breath, step away, laugh at the situation, and try again. Always trying; knowing it's not up to us.

LOVE

Love is a desire and a duty. We all want to be loved. Yet somehow it is hard to offer others the same courtesy. When we love well, all is well — and all will be well. When we struggle to extend our love to another, that's when we have to start paying attention. This is where the big prize is.

We want to be special, loveable, and impress others. So how do you do that? By doing something most people seem incapable of doing. By stepping up to the plate and seeking to love, when we really think we can't and we try nonetheless, that is when we are doing it, loving when it seems impossible, when most people walk away. Imagine that!

There was a real moment of realisation for me when I was once walking across a station hall on my way to work. An angry-looking man walked in the opposite direction. I tried to ignore him as he walked past, a little voice in my head saying *nasty little piece of work*, but then he looked up with a face of worry and confusion and asked me if I knew from which platform the next train to Amsterdam would leave. I looked into the face of a man, just like me. I told him which platform he was looking for and he thanked me with a gentle smile of gratitude. I saw a beautiful, sacred light. I was shocked. In my putrid judgemental head I had dismissed another human being based on massive assumptions . . . How often had I done this before? How many times a day? How many times have I passed up the opportunity to meet God in the other?

VULNERABILITY

To be vulnerable is to be willing to accept our insignificance. To enter the space of vulnerability is an experience of the great *letting go*. The paradox of this *letting go* is that as soon as we go past its threshold — where we share our weaknesses — it is experienced as a strength.

Vulnerability is the conduit of connection. When we show up in our full humanity we become meaningful to others. We make all the difference by just being who we truly are.

Stuck

middle aged
attached to my routine
hopeless in rigidity

let go my friend
life, just a breath
savour it

middle aged
committed to trying
smiling at my stupidity

Receive

stop
don't push
hang back

not forcing
takes courage

see it as an art
hone it
stay with it

Doubt

our secret weapon
need not
worry us

simply necessary
not pleasant
yet possible
to befriend

lack of it carries
undefined risk

without it
we go static
become less open
more alone

3 or 4?

Three is less than four; it is also the number for the spiritual. Three is an odd number; stable yet open to being destabilised — a three-legged table is very different from a four-legged one. Four is the number of the cardinal points and this even number can help us to navigate our journey.

So which one do you choose? Three, because deep down you intuit that in the end it's all about the spiritual, and isn't less more? Four, because you are a practical person? Why the dilemma? Why let yourself be sucked into one or the other? Choose both! The spiritual life is nothing if it's not applied. If we receive wisdom, we must use it, give it out, pass it on.

The challenge of our human existence is the art of right living; this is about creation, about making it real. Leadership is about raising the bar for oneself and everyone else. For that we require a both-and mindset. It's not quite the same as having your cake and eating it, because ultimately that turns out to be fallacious. When we go for both three *and* four we marry the two options and we choose to bridge the divide.

DEATH
AND AFTER

And a voice spoke to Ila and said: *Go out and tell people.*

Tell them what?

Go out.

And tell them?

Yes, go out, tell, and trust that you will have the words.

But I don't even know . . .

Then just go and trust — leaving the telling for later.

And Ila went out and told the people. And they liked to listen to her, even though it wasn't always clear what she was on about. And as she went out, her trust grew and her commitment became more disciplined — almost effortless. And as her message became clearer to her it started to land more with the people.

Her story was not hers; it was the story of the people. Ila was simply the vessel through which the words came to the people — their own truth, values, and purpose.

The going was good and the going was not so good. The clearer the message became to Ila the more unrest she felt among her audience. But it was so clear.

Is what I am telling clear to you?

All too clear.

Then why was there such unrest?

Ila was sitting in a bar. To her right there was an envelope. Who had put it there? She opened it: *Leave or die.* Ila ran, left town, and sought refuge in a remote village in the mountains. Rooms to let, safe harbour, time to reflect.

Night. Ila is wide awake. She looks at the wooden ceiling. Had a voice really spoken to her? It didn't matter, she had trusted and she had told the story. Why did she go out and tell the story? A story that everyone seemed to know when she spoke it. And why had they got unsettled as it got clearer — more true. She heard the great silence and waited for its revelation:

The truth is frightening. Truth is by its very essence unequivocally clear about what we ought to do. And this may mean giving up what we have and allowing new unknown things to arise. Giving things up is like dying. All our attachments are little lives, little parts of us. When we have to give them up — let them go, a part of us dies. And when we are confronted by the idea of death we think of the end, followed by nothing. Yet each time we let go of something, it simply creates space for new things to take their place. Somehow we always want to skip death, even though there is a new beginning beyond. The phoenix rises from the ashes like never before.

She had played her part and had experienced the consequences. She would recover and go out again. No longer fearing death but embracing the possibility of new lives beyond. *Leaving* would be dying.

HOW TO GET THERE

Buy a guide, read a book, listen to podcasts. Be successful, you can do it! Here's how . . . I also have important advice that will make the difference: stop looking for the answers, solutions, and certainties. Enjoy the process of finding out what makes you tick. Look for your very own, unique way.

I can hear you say, *But surely we can't all go around finding ourselves? No work would get done.* What work? The work you don't like doing? The work you do like doing? Either way you are not looking in the mirror. Maybe it's good to remember that there are more people out there who think they don't have a choice than there are who think that they do. It is quieter on the other side. I am not pretending I am on the other side continuously; I try to go there as often as I can, which is still far too seldom, but I try.

How others do it is not how you will do it or can possibly do it. Save time by not listening to clever people who make money telling you how to acquire mastery, attain success and earn a billion dollars, and use it instead to gently find your way. *What do you really want?*

When you are successful, you will be financially independent. Great, and what will that bring me? *You will be free.* Right. Why not be free now? Why wait for the money?

I am not free, because I am still fighting with myself. The spiritual battle: the hardest of them all. What is liberation? When I truly open myself, when what I want becomes irrelevant and when I can say yes to everyone and everything else.

We place our moments of success and freedom in the future to justify the life we don't want to lead. We dream up caveats that separate us from revelation, not realising that once we overcome each caveat new ones will continue to emerge.

HENK

You are no longer here and still with me almost every day. I had never imagined meeting someone like you; had hoped it, perhaps. God led me to you, I am sure of it. Seemingly, out of nothing came the desire to meet a member of your profession. I had never met one before. I wasn't even part of a church or any kind of religion. It just came to me. Several times over a period of some months, I think. After a while I felt a duty to respond to the knocking at my door.

A friend gave me your name. I rang you and told you. You said, *Well in that case we had better meet, right?* We met two weeks later. You poured your signature Lapsang Souchong. You received me with such gentleness, listening, simply. You said to just call if I wanted to visit again, an open hand outstretched. The next time we met was six months later; then three; then it became monthly.

I had never met a man like you, monumental in your quietness, your silence, your attentiveness, your presence. You rarely spoke, yet invited deep dialogue to take place. You saw me, *walked* with me, without judgement. I learnt from you without instruction. You let me dig for truth, my truth. You never suggested believing, never even spoke of God, yet you led me to Him. Or did He lead me to you, so that I could find Him through you, you truly His vessel?

In my time of discernment you told me to wait, intimated to hold off. You said there was no need to join — *you are part of it already.*

One day, I came to see you and was met by a look of lostness. Hair dishevelled, not your usual suave self. They wanted to celebrate your anniversaries of 60 years in the brotherhood and 50 years as a priest. You were distraught, looked cornered. Being the centre of attention, so not your thing. That day changed our relationship. That day you had decided to open the door and to let me meet you as another human being. You showed me the whole of you. It only made me respect you more. That day we became companions, fellow travellers. Later, when the celebrations took place, you had prepared yourself; you beamed in gratitude and delight, and you let it all happen. It was an act of service on your part. You were all about service; *love and service in everything.*

I asked you when you found God and you said, *He's always right here beside me, always has been,* as you nodded over your left shoulder. You were so solid in that awareness; solidly and humbly living this reality.

Six years after we first met I called you to tell you that I was ready. You said, *I am so grateful to hear this!* You had patiently waited, had wanted me to come to my own conclusions. I was your last liturgical act. You were loving and serene and it was a sacred moment for all in attendance.

A year later you rang. *I am calling to say goodbye.* You were grateful, there was nothing left for you to do here anymore. You stopped eating and drinking and waited for Him to come and fetch you. No fanfare, carefully considered, simple.

You are no longer here and still with me almost every day. I light a candle to remind me of your light.

SELF-LOVE

Love is the self-emptying process of dissolving the *I* in *the Other.* When we love, we act with purity and our intention is to create harmony for whom we direct our love toward. Love comes in different guises: motherly love, fraternal love, neighbourly love, lovers' love . . . Yet its underlying quality is the desire to give freely and without expectation.

Loving yourself is the same as loving others. Selfless love is in a way not possible. If we love Creation, everything that is, we must by definition love ourselves, as we are part of that creation.

You Are not that Important

Gone the need for recognition
success now common good

paying forward the trust
trust once placed in you

calibrate your inner compass
move from source
from stillness
and knowing

you ask questions

to unlock

not to make you look good

through knowing innocence

you create safe space

truly in service

indispensable in your expendability

you are free

UNRESOLVED

A train driver and still a young man when he fell off a locomotive onto the tracks. He fractured his spine in several places and never fully recovered, spending the rest of his life leaning on his elbows to alleviate the pain. He never complained.

A soldier and still a young man, he served his country in good faith. The reality was complex and he returned disillusioned and ashamed. He never complained.

I wasn't told these stories about his life. He told me different stories, easier ones. Looking back, he felt like a trapped animal. He was a gentle man, who, without warning, could explode in a fit of rage. He never spoke about his feelings. It must have been lonely. Unable to access the disappointment, shame and helplessness. Lifelong suffering. He never complained.

I'm grateful to see my children comfortable expressing their emotions. Release comes through the acknowledgement and acceptance of our brokenness, our feelings of fear, anxiety, shame, unworthiness, sadness and anger. For my grandfather these burdens remained unresolved.

HUT PAN

I would sometimes stay with her. There were no toys, nothing to play with. It was the house my father had grown up in. There were no mementos of that time. There was a Persian rug on the dining table that smelt of cigar and cigarette ashes, a side dresser with a crystal presentation dish, violets in the window sill, sometimes begonias. It was the home of a long-time widow and time had come to a standstill here.

I should have been bored stiff staying there, but all I can remember is sacred dreamtime. Stories that she made up as she went along, adventures she'd send me on, letting me eat my lunch in the back of the garden in the hollow of a big shrub, serving my food in a bowl she called the *hut pan*.

My elder cousins had spent time with her when she was

younger and had more energy. She took them on bicycle rides and baked them pancakes over a woodfire in the forest. With me she did things more slowly. It had a sense of mystery to it. At home again, her house was in another world.

My grandmother made me feel special. She did this simply by being fully present, fully with me. Perhaps, this is the power of poverty. She knew what it meant to have just the present moment. No money, no fancy clothes, no books, no holidays. Just the company of others.

WAR

We are sharing our house with a family from Ukraine. They are wonderful. They are safe here, but it's not home. They have family who have stayed behind. They worry about the shellings, seeing their country being destroyed and pillaged. The upset and grief is heart-rending. How do we attend to that? How can we hold them in a way that is supportive, bears witness? Life goes on, things become normal. Is that okay? It feels wrong, and it is necessary to be able to carry the hardship, to get on with life.

Our friends apply for jobs. Promises are made. We are so glad to see them sparkle with hope, with the chance to start building again. Then the job falls through. The commitment turned out to be rather light. Offering someone who has lost almost everything something to look forward to, to believe in, and then crush that hope a couple of days later? How callous can you get?

It's not easy to truly understand what others feel. Yet the quality with which we do this is our only hope of real connection. We must make time for it. Do I know how it feels to be hurt? Can I remind myself that the other feels pain with the same depth? Truly imagining the feelings of another, realising there is no difference between me and you, leads to a fundamentally different response. I start to know, to truly understand, that what happens to the other happens to me. When you are being attacked, then I, also, I am under siege. When you lose a friend, I lose a friend.

And then there is the paradox that your pain is not my suffering; it is simply my duty to *feel into* that suffering to enable me to help you in carrying it. I must grieve with you and for you, but not for me. This is not about me, it's about you. My actions are based on that piece of you that I know is also in me.

OLD

My hands ache. I think it's arthritis. I am overcome with grief. Sadness of life slipping away from me. The irreversible process of ageing. Fear of death? I say I am okay with getting older. In fact, I can see the beauty in an ageing body and mind. Yet, at the first clear sign of age I shrink back. I don't want the pain! I don't want to be decrepit. I just want to age in a beautiful way.

My hands ache. I am not as strong as I used to be. My body is showing signs of weakness. I am becoming less dependable. I cannot carry as much as I used to. My sense of control needs reviewing. Rationally, yes, of course, no man is an island — easy. But now I am becoming dependent in the daily practical sense. I see an image of an old man in his kitchen who cannot open a jar of jam; wait it's me!

My hands ache. And I am terrified. I cannot tell you exactly why. It may have something to do with the sense of unpredictability or losing control; where will this leave me? Will I be able to continue to work? Will I be able to sustain this hard-wearing schedule?

My hands ache. I see my children grow towards adulthood; shining with health and fitness. And I cannot keep up.

My hands ache. I should rejoice! This is my body forcing me to start depending on something beyond the physical faculty. I must start becoming a little wiser; start using my experience in service to others. My physical contribution is becoming less relevant; others are much more effective in that space. Wonderful. Am I ready? Dare I trust it?

My hands ache. I feel very lonely. I realise how little empathy I have had for people with serious illnesses. I feel so alone.

My hands ache. Where is God in that? What is He trying to tell me? Slow down? Too easy. Don't use your hands? Yeah, right. Give over? Give over . . . Can I actually do that? Very difficult for me. I am not supposed to give over, to be weak, to admit that I need help. Say it: I need help.

I can't open the jam jar. Can you help me, please?

Winter Sea

Set off
before sunrise
ready
to encounter
Nature

slight breeze
park quiet
not so early
the world sleeps

down steps
see her
new friend
or old?

move forward
colder now
unease

keep going
change
jump off wall
short prayer
and in — waist deep
gulp for air
in I go

submersion
eyes open
twelve, thirteen, fourteen . . .
strokes before resurfacing

rebirth
no regret
just gratitude
and wonder

SEEKERS

Within us there is an ongoing conversation around what matters and what does not. The sad thing is that we spend most of our time on what matters less; we do what we feel is expected of us rather than the things that are meaningful to us.

When I say meaningful I am not talking about the personal satisfaction of needs; I am talking about being the person I know I can be, my true self. When I picture how I would like to respond to someone asking for help, I see myself as kind, considerate, conscientious, intelligent, inquisitive, decisive, and so on. In every situation, we try to act according to what we think is the right way. When we lose our balance due to the pressure we perceive, we start misjudging situations and behaving differently compared to the being and responding we are capable of when we are in a healthy balance. Under pressure, I risk losing my composure, it then becomes harder to hear what people need from me, let alone that I can even be generous in that situation. From the outside, these things are obvious, but when we are in the middle of it, we can easily lose perspective on what really matters. Clear examples of this are sensations of flow and of connection with self and others; when these occur we are experiencing our highest personal potential, a magical sensation.

What I describe here applies not only to situations, but to our lives as a whole. In the heat of living, we lose connection to our compass; the compass that points toward what is meaningful to us. When we have gone totally off track, when we realise we are lost and we wonder how we can reset, how to get back to the way we want to be, act, and live. For this it is fundamental to ask for help. As soon as we do that there is the possibility of connection, the spiritual food that sustains our attempts to grow.

Working towards this ideal way of living is spirituality. Our ongoing efforts to craft ourselves towards an ever-evolving ideal of self is what makes us develop. This dynamic is what we commit to when we decide to become seekers.

EPILOGUE

One evening I asked my wife to read these pages aloud so I could hear them from the outside, and listening, a space of stillness came over me: *Do you know what? I don't think I wrote these pages.* She answered: *I don't think you did either.* I feel that something has been poured out of me that requires presence and availability and has not come from me alone. I think this is the true fruit of this book for me.

ABOUT THE
AUTHOR

Jake Esman is a leadership coach and facilitator. He is intrigued by the human condition of organisations and our capacity to improve this. He believes that the key to sustainable performance lies in our compassion — for ourselves, for others, and for the world we live in.

In 2020 he co-founded The Way Over, a leadership development advisory firm.

He is an Oblate of Quarr Abbey and lives on the Isle of Wight with his wife, Annabel, and their three children.